KART RACERS

Alison G. Norville

Enslow Publishers, Inc.
40 Industrial Road
Box 398
Berkeley Heights, NJ 07922
USA
http://www.enslow.com

Library of Congress Cataloging-in-Publication Data
Norville, Alison G.
  Kart racers / Alison G. Norville.
    p. cm. — (Kid racers)
  Includes bibliographical references and index.
  Summary: "High interest book for reluctant readers containing action packed photos
and stories of the hottest go-karts and races for kids, discussing which karts qualify,
how they are built and raced, who the best drivers are, what to look for in a kart,
safety, good sportsmanship, and how racing activities can be a good part of family
life"—Provided by publisher.
  ISBN 978-0-7660-3482-2
  1. Karting—Juvenile literature. I. Title.
  GV1029.5.N67 2010
  796.7'6—dc22
                                    2009020786

ISBN 978-0-7660-3754-0 (paperback)

Printed in the United States of America

102009 Lake Book Manufacturing, Inc., Melrose Park, IL

10 9 8 7 6 5 4 3 2 1

To Our Readers:
We have done our best to make sure all Internet addresses in this book were active
and appropriate when we went to press. However, the author and the publisher have
no control over and assume no liability for the material available on those Internet
sites or on other Web sites they may link to. Any comments or suggestions can be sent
by e-mail to comments@enslow.com or to the address on the back cover.
    Any stunts shown in this book have been performed by experienced drivers and
should not be attempted by beginners.

♻ Enslow Publishers, Inc., is committed to printing our books on recycled paper.
The paper in every book contains 10% to 30% post-consumer waste (PCW). The cover
board on the outside of each book contains 100% PCW. Our goal is to do our part to
help young people and the environment too!

Adviser: *Jack Hoegerl, board member of the International Karting Federation, chairman
of the 2-Cycle Tech Committee*

Cover Photo Credit: On Track Promotions/Todd McCall
Interior Photo Credits: Action Sports Photos/Bruce Walls, p. 30; Alamy/Stephen
Roberts, p. 10; Alamy/London Aerial Photo Library, p. 11; Alamy/INSADCO
Photography, p. 18; Alamy/Buzz Pictures, p. 19; Alamy/Joe Fox, pp. 21, 23 (top);
Alamy/Giovanni Mereghetti, p. 22; Alamy/Joe Fox Motorsport, p. 27; AP Photo, p. 31;
AP Photo/Shuji Kajiyama, p. 37; Courtesy Of New Castle Motorsports Park, p. 29;
Double Vision Photography/Carl Barnes, pp. 5, 6, 12, 20, 23 (bottom), 24, 25, 34, 25;
Expressions Fine Photography/Curt Davis, pp. 9, 17, 41; Fotolia/Nicola Gavin, p. 26;
Getty Images/Dave Sandford, p. 32; Getty Images/Philip Brown, p. 36; Jim Hall Kart
Racing School, pp. 42, 43; iStockphoto.com/Kativ, p. 38 (background); iStockphoto.
com/Gabriela Schaufelberger, p. 39; iStockphoto.com/Andy Cook Illustration, p. 44;
David Lee Photography, pp. 1, 4, 28, 40; Courtesy of Andy McGavic, pp. 7, 13; On Track
Promotions/Todd McCall, pp. 15, 16; Courtesy of Road America Karting Club, p. 33;
SuperStock, Inc./SuperStock, p. 8.

Contents

IS IT A DREAM?

Imagine that you're a kart racer. Now is the big moment—the last lap of the Karting World Championship at Daytona International Speedway in Florida.

You dive left into the infield on NASCAR turn 1. Your competition, number 19, is strong on the straightaways. You have to pass number 19 before you dart back onto the oval. You take the outside line. Then you swing hard to the left, with just a quick touch on the brake to set up the next right-hand turn. You barrel ahead, wide open, and leave number 19 in the dust.

Speed carries you up the bank of NASCAR turn 2. As you follow the track along the shore of Lake Lloyd, you hear 19 gaining on you. On the steep slope of NASCAR turn 3, he shoots in front! You duck into his draft as you take the final corner. When you catch sight of the flagman, you slingshot around. Side by side, you and 19 dash the final 50 feet. You have him by a nose when the flagman waves the checker.

You won! Was it a dream?

High Banks

Daytona International Speedway's turns are banked 31 degrees. The steep bank lets drivers take the sharp corners without touching their brake pedals.

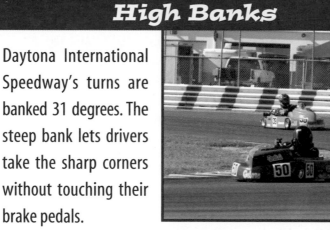

Banked turns at Daytona let racers go fast, but they also keep karters safe.

Join the Club

Winning a race at Daytona is unforgettable. You join an elite club. The club's legendary members include Richard Petty, Dale Earnhardt, and Kevin Harvick.

IT CAN COME TRUE!

You don't have to be a spectator watching kart races from the grandstands. You can drive—not just in your yard or at an amusement park, but on a racetrack against other racers like you.

There are hundreds of kart tracks in the United States. You can probably find one within an hour of your home. Tracks hold organized races for drivers from the age of five and up.

Racers can practice year-round at G & J Kartway in Camden, Ohio. Movie star Tom Cruise went to a driving school here to prepare for his role in the movie *Days of Thunder*.

Karting is a good way to start racing. It can be a family hobby, or it can be the first step in a professional driving career. There are karting groups for kids of almost any age, experience level, and budget.

Karting is an inexpensive and fun way to join the world of motor sports.

It's Not Just for Grown-ups

About 45 percent of kart racers in the United States are under the age of 18. Karting is the ideal sport for kid racers!

The Big Leagues

The International Kart Federation (IKF) and the World Karting Association (WKA)—the major kart racing organizations—have about 15,000 racing members.

Early kart racers rev up their engines at the starting line. In the background, fans wait at the first turn.

KARTING BACK IN THE DAY

Art Ingels was a race car builder in California. In 1956, Ingels designed and built the original go-kart. Other people saw his kart and created their own. Go Kart Manufacturing, the first business to sell go-karts, opened in 1958. Early mechanics borrowed gasoline engines from lawn mowers or tractors. The first company to make engines specifically for go-karts was called McCulloch. The company used its chain saw motor as a model for its special kart engine.

The first kart races were held in parking lots. Tracks just for go-karts came later. Soon, drivers decided to make official rules for the new sport. They formed the International Kart Federation in 1957. The federation's rules helped make karting safe and fair.

When races were held in parking lots, safety was a problem. Karts could spin out right into a group of spectators!

Dropping the Go

Racers dropped the *go* from the name *go-kart* long ago. The sport is now called karting, and the vehicles are called karts. Today, "go-karts" are considered toys.

No Playing Around

Don't be fooled. Early go-karts were not toys. Serious drivers competed in these pioneering machines.

KARTING NOW

Gone are the days of building a kart in your garage. A lot of careful engineering goes into sleek, modern racing machines.

Kart manufacturing is a billion-dollar business worldwide. Karts, engines, and tires are sent to the United States from all over the globe. A chassis (pronounced CHA-see) might come from North Carolina or Australia. Some engines come from Italy. Most tires are made in Japan.

You don't need to travel around the world to buy your kart. There might be a kart shop near you. You can check the Internet for online stores. Most shops also have mail-order catalogs.

Today's racers have many track choices. There are three basic types of kart tracks— speedways, sprint tracks, and road race courses. Karting speedways are oval shaped. They may be paved or made of dirt. Sprint tracks are paved tracks with both left and right turns. Road race courses are the longest. Sports cars also use them.

It's Your Choice

This track is located in the country setting of Kimbolton, England.

Most NASCAR races are held on oval speedways, either dirt or paved. Formula One fans go for the winding curves of the sprint and road race courses.

At a kart race, the action in the pits can be just as exciting as the action on the track.

YOU'RE HOOKED . . . WHAT'S NEXT?

You've gone to a kart race. The action, sounds, and excitement have made you a motor sports fan. Now, how do you get started as a new racer?

Walk through the pits at a race. Talk to the drivers and their crews. Ask about the right racing classes for your age group. Find out if you and your family have the mechanical skills to work on a kart.

Then stop by the track office for other useful information. Sign up for the track's mailing list. Collect copies of the rule book and newsletter.

If possible, try sitting in a kart. Do you feel comfortable? You might even take a test drive. Many clubs have a "fun run" at the end of the day. They let rookies borrow a kart for a trial run. Give it a try and see if karting is really for you.

The first time you drive a kart, you might be surprised by its power. Be light on the throttle at first!

Don't Be Shy

When you walk around the pits at a race, stop and ask questions. Karters love their sport. They will talk about it for hours.

BEFORE YOUR FIRST RACE

Preparation is the key to winning. Learn all you can before you go to your first race.

Search the Internet for trade shows. At these events, people showcase new products at booths in a large building. Also look for swap meets, where karters sell used equipment at bargain prices.

When you go, talk to the people who sell karting supplies. Many companies have brochures with excellent information. Trade shows and swap meets are great places to find a builder to work on your kart engine. In addition, experts often give classes at these events. They share tips on mechanics and driving.

Some kart clubs have special schools for beginners in the off-season. This is a chance to learn from experienced karters. The club may assign mentors to help rookies during their first season.

Learn from the Pros

At a trade show, watch carefully and never be afraid to ask questions. The presenters are glad to answer. They all remember their first time racing. Then, when you go home, read all the information you collected.

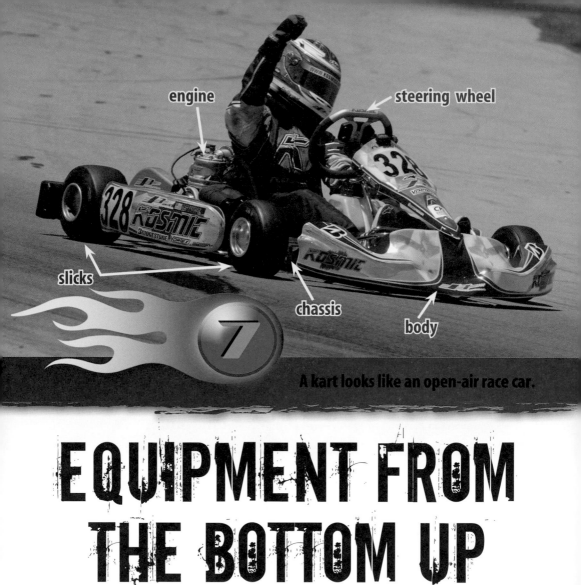

engine

steering wheel

slicks

chassis

body

A kart looks like an open-air race car.

EQUIPMENT FROM THE BOTTOM UP

Are you ready to buy your first kart? Your first purchase is the chassis, the kart's steel-tube frame. A sprint kart chassis is best for beginners. In this kind of kart, the racer drives sitting up. A sprinter can race on most tracks.

The other kind of chassis is called either enduro or lay-down. The driver lies on his

back. This reduces wind resistance, so the kart goes faster. Enduro karts are used only in road races on long tracks.

Next, you will need special tires. Karts use slicks— tires without treads.

Enduro karts are for experienced drivers. Enduro races can last up to 45 minutes!

Their soft rubber grips the surface of the track without slowing you down.

Some karts have fiberglass bodies. These bodies give the kart an aerodynamic shape. This makes it slip cleanly through the air.

Finally, you can't go fast without good brakes to help you stop. All karts use a disc brake on the rear axle. Karts in some racing classes need front brakes, too.

A High-tech Machine

An amazing amount of engineering goes into making a chassis. A kart has no springs or shock absorbers. The steel tubing must be flexible enough not to crack when speeding through the curves. It also must be stiff enough to keep all four wheels on the ground in the turns.

POWER UP!

You've bought most of your kart parts—but you've got no power! Now it's time to choose an engine.

A four-cycle engine is a good choice for a beginning karter. Four-cycles are like lawn mower engines. They provide a top speed of 90 miles per hour (mph).

An experienced racer might choose a two-cycle engine made for racing. Two-cycles allow karts to reach speeds of 130 mph. Some karts, known as Superkarts, can go 160 mph.

Shown here is a four-cycle, 100cc kart engine.

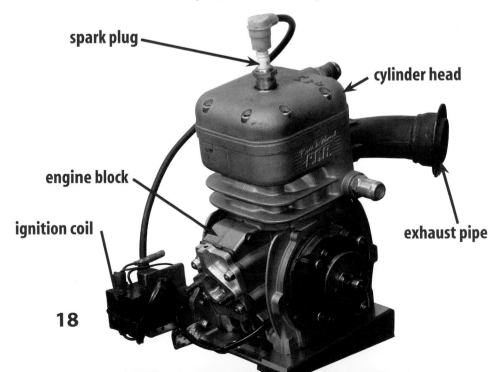

spark plug

cylinder head

engine block

ignition coil

exhaust pipe

Next, you'll need an engine gauge, also called a tach-temp gauge. This instrument shows how well the engine is working. The gauge must have two readouts. The tachometer—tach for short—tells how many times the piston inside the engine is revolving each minute. This is called the revolutions per minute (rpm).

The gauge also must have a thermometer that shows the temperature, or temp, of the engine. A speedometer is also interesting to have, but it's not necessary.

The tach-temp gauge tells a kart driver how healthy the engine is.

To move the power from the engine to the wheels, you need a clutch. There are two kinds of clutches: axle and engine. Check the rules for your racing class, and then select the kind of clutch that is required.

Broken In, Not Broken Down

It's okay to buy used equipment. Look for clean, well-kept parts. At the end of the racing season, many drivers sell used equipment as they upgrade for the next year.

FINISHING TOUCHES

Before you're ready to race, you need a few more specialty karting items. Just like Indy cars, karts do not have built-in starters. You must have a starter to turn on the engine.

Different tracks require different gears to adjust your power. Ask around at your local track, and buy the correct gears.

Karts are very low to the ground. You will need a stand to raise the kart while you work on it.

The garages at Daytona Kart Week buzz with mechanical activity.

Nearly every kart racing class requires a specific exhaust pipe. Check your track's rule book for the correct pipe.

Almost everything else you need at the track is in a common tool kit. Organize your tools so they are easy to find.

An exhaust pipe lets out burned gas from inside a kart's engine.

Most drivers use a little wagon to carry their starter system and important tools around the pits. You don't want to waste time and energy looking for misplaced things.

Race Day Checklist

Make sure you have all these items before you head to the track:

- ✔ complete kart
- ✔ kart stand
- ✔ starter
- ✔ extra spark plugs
- ✔ tool kit
- ✔ gasoline tanks
- ✔ spray oil
- ✔ spray cleaners
- ✔ brake fluid

- ✔ hand cleaner
- ✔ flashlight
- ✔ fire extinguisher
- ✔ track rule book
- ✔ tire pressure gauge
- ✔ twisty wire ties
- ✔ nuts and bolts
- ✔ clutch oil
- ✔ safety wire

- ✔ stopwatch
- ✔ clipboard or notebook
- ✔ tape measure
- ✔ duct tape
- ✔ gears
- ✔ spare tires
- ✔ pit wagon
- ✔ paper towels

A young kart rider is all geared up for safe racing in a helmet, driving suit, gloves, and boots.

SUIT UP FOR SAFETY

A professional driver's uniform is not just for advertising. It is vital safety equipment. Just like the pros, what you wear may make the difference between life and death.

The most important piece of safety gear is your helmet. It protects your brain. Karts don't

have windshields, so you need a helmet that covers your whole face. It must have the latest Snell approval rating.

Racers under the age of sixteen have to wear an SFI-approved chest protector. Young bodies have soft bones that bend. If you hit the steering wheel in a crash, your ribs could squeeze your heart. A chest protector will keep your heart safe.

A racer's helmet protects him from dust as well as head injuries.

Sprinters must wear a foam neck collar. This safety device helps protect the neck and collarbones.

A driving suit does more than look cool. It helps reduce road rash if your body drags against the track. Driving suits are made of strong fabric or leather, with padding on the elbows and knees.

To guard your hands, you have to wear gloves. Look for racing gloves with padding on the tops of the hands and grips on the palms.

Check Before You Buy

Never buy a used helmet. A new one is always stronger. Look inside a helmet to find its Snell rating (right).

FINAL SAFETY CHECK

You're all geared up and ready to race. Your final safety stop is called pre-race safety tech. A trained inspector will check five areas of your equipment:

1. Brakes—The inspector pushes the pedal to see how well the brakes work. No fluid may leak from the lines. There can be no cracks in the disc. He checks all nuts and bolts.

2. Throttle—After the pedal is pushed, it must spring back to the off position. He checks all nuts and bolts.

Officials carefully inspect a kart to make sure it is clear to race.

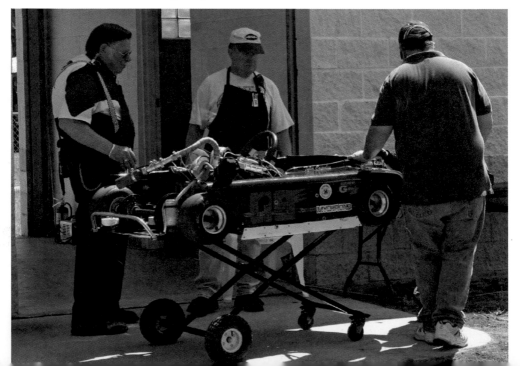

3. *Steering*—He turns the steering wheel to make sure the front wheels turn. He checks all nuts and bolts.

4. *Fuel system*—All the plastic fuel lines must be fastened tightly with safety wire or a wire tie. Nothing may leak.

5. *Helmet*—The inspector checks the helmet's Snell rating.

If the inspector finds anything wrong with your kart, he sends you back to fix it. When you pass inspection, you get a sticker on your kart and on your helmet. This shows that you are ready to race. No kart is allowed on the track without a sticker proving that it passed safety tech.

Wired for Safety

Karts vibrate a lot. Even a tight nut can turn off its bolt. To prevent this from happening, drill a tiny hole into the nut and the bolt. After the nut is secured, slip safety wire or a cotter key through the hole. Then the nut cannot come off. Kart inspectors check the bolts for this safety feature. Shown here is a safety wire on the brake caliper.

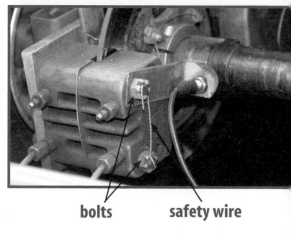

bolts   safety wire

THAT'S WHY IT'S CALLED AN ACCIDENT

You passed pre-tech, and you're wearing safety gear. You're safe, aren't you? Yes, but you can't prevent all accidents. Sometimes parts break, and unplanned events happen. Karting is a competitive sport. You need to do everything possible to prevent an accident.

Check your tires each time you go out. A worn tire may blow out and spin you into the path of another driver.

If you break down, move your kart off the racing surface. Wait for help in a safe spot away from the action.

Always keep an eye on the corner workers—the officials standing at the corners of the track. When an official waves a yellow flag, expect trouble ahead.

Racers slow down immediately when they see a yellow flag.

A group of kart racers gets in a minor crash on an Ireland track. Accidents do happen!

Never drive recklessly. Unsafe driving causes deadly accidents. Karts can't take bumping and pushing like NASCAR autos, because they don't have strong bodies. Treat other drivers the way you expect to be treated.

Finally, be confident. Most crashes can be avoided if you stay safe and follow the rules.

What Does That Flag Mean?

A green flag starts the race, and a black and white checkered flag ends it. What about the others? Learn to read all the signal flags on page 44. That is how track officials communicate with you.

NEW CASTLE MOTORSPORTS PARK

New Castle Motorsports Park in Indiana is the favorite sprint kart track of many racers. Former Indy car driver and Formula Atlantic champion Mark Dismore, Sr., opened the track in 2004.

Dismore says, "This has been a labor of love. I planned to build the nicest track anywhere. It makes me feel good when people from all over the world tell me it is their favorite track."

More than sixty karts line up at the beginning of a 200-mile endurance race at New Castle Motorsports Park. This three-hour-long race features pit stops and driver changes. Drivers have to be fifteen or older to enter the event.

This aerial photo shows the dramatic turns of New Castle's track. The main track is 1 mile long and 28 feet wide.

The New Castle track is used for karting races from 0.5 to 1.5 miles long. It has many thrilling turns and hills.

Cars also race at New Castle. Mini Coopers average 77 mph, and Corvettes average 89 mph. Believe it or not, karts are the fastest, at 93 mph!

A Luxury Track

The New Castle track rents garage space to kart teams during races. Working from a garage is a luxury for any racer.

GEORGIA KARTING KOMPLEX

Georgia Karting Komplex is popular with dirt-kart racers from the southern United States. This track is a quarter of a mile long. It is flat, with low banking on the corners. Here, the fastest karts reach top speeds of 80 mph.

At the Georgia Karting Komplex , racers face a slightly slippery surface: dirt. Dirt-kart races are often held at night. This is another challenge.

Great care goes into preparing a dirt track. A special clay is ground fine and then spread on the track. Machines pack the clay and roll it smooth. Before a race, the track is sprinkled with water to make the racing surface stronger.

Sprint karts race at the Georgia Karting Komplex nearly every weekend. As many as seven hundred entries fill the air with dust and let out the roar of Briggs and Stratton engines.

In the Footsteps of the Pros

The sport of dirt-kart racing came from early stock car racing. Competition is just as fierce. Today, dirt racing is a training ground for NASCAR drivers.

Stock cars compete at the NASCAR Sportsman Race in 1954.

The track at Road America was built in 1955. It has been improved many times since then, but it still has the same shape.

ROAD AMERICA

Each year, hundreds of road racers from around the country go to Wisconsin to run at Road America. The track is more than 4 miles long, with 14 turns and steep hills. This course challenges even the best drivers to their limits.

Road America boasts that it is the fastest permanent road course in the world. Many kinds of vehicles race here. Top speeds on the front straightaway reach 200 mph. Average lap speeds are slower. Cars have average lap speeds of 135 mph. Motorcycles average 110 mph. Karts are not far behind, at 107 mph.

World Famous

Road America is a world-famous racetrack. More than 350 motor sports events are held there each year.

To the Max

The Kink, one of the most difficult turns at Road America, tests both the driving skills of the racer and the strength of the kart. Shown below is the Briggs & Stratton Motorplex, a part of the Road America track that is open to both karts and dirt bikes.

16

Drafting is one of the smartest strategies in kart racing. Soon, kart 89 can slingshot ahead of kart 13.

TO FINISH FIRST, FIRST YOU MUST FINISH

Winning takes hard work, not luck or tricks. Here are some tips that will help make you a true karting champ.

First, always arrive prepared on race day. Don't waste time at the track doing things that you could have done at home.

Learning the track is a major key to success. Be ready on the grid for each practice round. During track time you'll discover your line—the quickest path around the track.

You've probably seen how NASCAR drivers draft. That means they line up behind each other on the track during a race in order to go faster. Drafting works with karts, too. This is a valuable skill to practice. Make friends with other drivers in your class. Planning to draft will help all of you go faster.

Controlling your kart's slide in the corners is important, too. Once you've learned a turn, you will know when to brake. More time on the gas pedal—and less time on the brake—means greater speed.

Finally, be patient. Expect to make mistakes. What matters is what you *do* when you make a mistake. Turn each mistake into a lesson.

Wheel Warm-up

Don't slide through a turn on your first lap of the day. Slick tires need to warm up before they can grip the track.

British Formula One driver Lewis Hamilton won his first karting championship when he was ten years old.

THE LITTLE LEAGUE OF MOTOR SPORTS

Just as professional baseball players often start out in Little League, many of today's professional race car drivers began in kart racing. Most Formula One racers, including the new star Lewis Hamilton, were karters. World champion

Michael Schumacher loves karting. He owns kart tracks and schools in Europe.

Many NASCAR greats came from karts. Darrell Waltrip, Tony Stewart, and Lake Speed all ran kart races. In fact, Speed returned to his roots and joined WKA's fastest sprint class. Now he races a shifter kart.

Marco Andretti grew up in a long-time racing family. They started him in karts. In 1997, Andretti finished second at his first kart race in Flemington, New Jersey. In less than ten years, he was driving Indy cars.

Danica Patrick, today's most famous woman racer, began kart racing in 1992 at Sugar River Raceway near Brodhead, Wisconsin. Patrick went on to win several national karting championships. T. J. Patrick, Danica's father, says, "Danica just couldn't wait to start racing. I made it a rule that if she was going to do this, she had to learn something every time she went onto the track."

Auto-racing star Danica Patrick celebrates her win at the Japan 300 race in April 2008. Patrick started her career by driving karts.

TRICK YOUR RIDE

No two karts look exactly the same. Lots of racers give their karts fancy paint jobs. Some look like tigers, while others are painted like dragons. One dentist painted a toothy grin on the front of his kart.

Another way to stand out is to name your team. Chose a name the sounds speedy, like Fast Cat Racing. Then have a print shop make decals for your kart.

Famed racer Conor Daly tricks his kart with a sleek paint job, decals, and company logos.

A sticker kit really brightens up a kart.

Perhaps they could have the shape of a running cat. You could get T-shirts printed with the same design for your family and crew.

Stripes are a cheaper way to jazz up your kart. Auto parts stores sell easy-to-use stripe kits in many colors. Be creative!

Sometimes a simple design is best. But the only limit is your imagination.

Team Colors

Bright colors and stripes make you stand out on the track. Your fans will see you easily in a pack.

Pro Decals

Decals make your kart look like a pro's. Most kart shops, racetracks, and businesses give away decals for free.

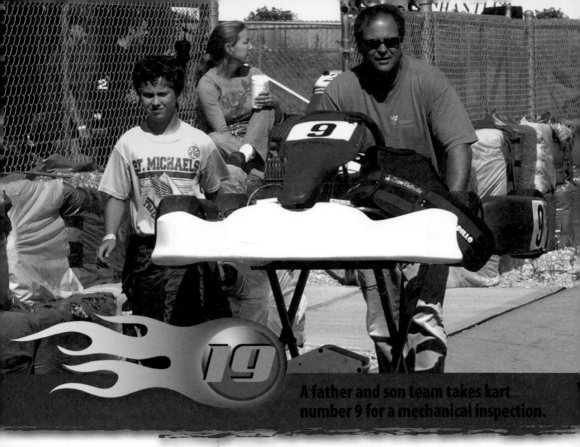

A father and son team takes kart number 9 for a mechanical inspection.

IT'S A FAMILY AFFAIR

Kart racing is more fun when the whole family is involved. Everyone can have a job on a family race team. One family member, the crew chief, takes care of the engine and other mechanical work. Other helpers are the record keeper, doctor, cook, and cheerleader. You are the assistant mechanic, as well as the driver.

A successful karting family works as a team. They all respect each other. At the end of the day, the whole crew feels good, knowing they all have done their best.

Keeping Track at the Track

It is important to keep exact records of your lap times—how long it takes to circle the track—both in practice and during a race. That is how you can tell if you're improving.

Getting It All There

As you can see, the sport of karting involves a lot of equipment! How are you going to bring all of your supplies to the racetrack? You'll see lots of different ways. Some race teams pack up the family minivan. Others have the newest toy hauler—a combination of a motor home and a garage.

This kid racer transports his equipment in a deluxe toy hauler.

BACK TO SCHOOL

Do you want to improve your karting skills? A driving school may be the answer.

The Jim Hall Kart Racing School in Oxnard, California is a good choice. It offers classes geared to your age and experience. The Parent and Child Program accepts kids from ages ten to fourteen. You will learn braking, starting, and driving in a safe setting.

The Jim Hall Kart Racing School was founded in 1982. Jim Hall II is a double World Kart Champion.

A Racing Education

Driving schools are a good way to sharpen your skills. The teachers watch you drive, evaluate your strengths, and help you improve your weaknesses. A driving school is expensive, but it can be worth it.

At the Jim Hall Kart Racing School, you can practice for hours without the crowds and pressures of a race.

Top of the Class

The Jim Hall Kart Racing School has had more than 40,000 students. Some of them became famous as racers, actors, or musicians. Famous Jim Hall graduates include NASCAR drivers Brett Bodine and Michael Waltrip, Olympic gold medalist Bruce Jenner, talk show host David Letterman, actor Kevin Spacey, and comedian Jerry Seinfeld.

LEARN THE FLAGS

Green—Beginning of the race; drivers are clear to speed up after a yellow flag

Blue—A faster racer is trying to pass; move over and allow them to pass

Red—Slow down completely and go back to the pits

White—Last lap of the race

Yellow—Slow down; trouble ahead

Black—Penalty; the driver who receives the wave must return to the pits

Black and white checkered—End of the race

GLOSSARY

aerodynamic—Able to slide through the air easily.

axle—The bar on which the rear wheels of a kart turn.

chassis—A metal frame that supports the body and engine of a kart or car.

clutch—A device for working the gears of an engine.

disc brake—A type of brake that grabs a round metal disc to stop a vehicle.

draft—A place behind a vehicle where there is lower wind resistance. Racers often ride in each other's drafts so they can go faster.

engineering—The field of using science and math to design machines.

four-cycle engine—A type of internal combustion engine used in karting and elsewhere. One stroke of every four is the power stroke. It is generally less powerful than a two-cycle engine, where the power stroke is every other stroke.

gears—Discs covered with teeth that connect and transfer the energy from a vehicle's engine to its wheels.

grid—The area where karts line up before going out on the track.

kink—A sharp bend or curve.

mechanics—People who work on engines and other parts of machines.

mentors—People who guide or teach others.

piston—A part of an engine that moves up and down within a tight sleeve in order to make the machine work.

pits—The areas where race teams work on their karts.

racing classes—Groups that race together because they have similar vehicles, engines, body weights, and ages.

rookies—Beginners; people who are just starting to learn something.

rpm—Revolutions per minute. Generally, the higher the RPM, the more energy the engine is producing.

SFI—A company that sets safety standards for motor vehicles based upon scientific testing.

shock absorbers—Parts of an automobile that make the ride feel smoother by absorbing, or taking up, bounces on a rough surface.

slicks—Tires that do not have treads.

Snell approval rating—A safety score that the Snell Memorial Foundation gives to helmets based upon scientific testing.

straightaways—Long sections of a racetrack between the corners.

throttle—The gas pedal of a vehicle.

treads—The grooved outer surfaces of a tire that allow it to grip the road.

wind resistance—The force of air against an object.

FURTHER READING

Books

David, Jack. *Go-Kart Racing.* Minneapolis, Minn.: Bellwether Media, 2008.

Gidley, Memo and Jeff Grist. *Karting: Everything You Need to Know.* St. Paul, Minn.: Motorbooks, 2006.

Herran, Joe and Ron Thomas. *Karting.* Philadelphia: Chelsea House, 2004.

Mello, Tara Baukus. *Danica Patrick.* New York: Chelsea House, 2007.

Web Sites

International Karting Federation—*Learn about the world's first kart racing organization.*
<www.ikfkarting.com>

World Karting Association—*Visit this site to learn more about organized kart races, rules, and stars of the sport.*
<www.worldkarting.com>

INDEX